The Keepsake Storm

CAMINO DEL SOL

A Latina and Latino Literary Series

The Keepsake Storm

POEMS BY Gina Franco

The University of Arizona Press

Tucson

The University of Arizona Press
© 2004 The Arizona Board of Regents
First Printing
All rights reserved

Library of Congress Cataloging-in-Publication Data
appear on the last printed page of this book.

British Library Cataloguing-in-Publication Data
A catalogue record for this book is available from
the British Library.

Publication of this book is made possible in part
by the proceeds of a permanent endowment
created with the assistance of a Challenge Grant
from the National Endowment for
the Humanities, a federal agency.

Chris, Glenda

tierra, ojos

Trystan

siempre las palabras, siempre

padre, madre,

padrastro, hermano,

cuñada, sobrinas

my love

But thought can with difficulty visit the intricate and
winding chambers which it inhabits. It is like a river whose
rapid and perpetual stream flows outwards—like one in dread
who speeds through the recesses of some haunted pile and
dares not look behind. . . . If it were possible to be where we
have been, vitally and indeed—if, at the moment of our
presence there, we could define the results of our experience—if
the passage from sensation to reflection—from a state of
passive perception to voluntary contemplation were not so
dizzying and so tumultuous, this attempt
would be less difficult.

—Percy Bysshe Shelley

Contents

ONE

It is difficult, says Plato, to find the parent and author
of the universe, and impossible when you have found him, that
you may declare him to anyone.

—Sir William Drummond

Fishing

You want real? Draw your thumbs along
the backbones of fossilized fish
and press your fingers into the brush
of vertebrae, the singular eyes, fronds
of fins. See? Self-portrait. Osteichthyes fanned
in accuracy, bone-hollows that are you
exactly, you perpetually, you
who thought yourself detached from sand,
salt, and cannibal rage. Now sit outside
this tank. Want in? Want to be sleek? Too bad.
But imagine being made that way. Whose reel,
you think, wouldn't relent before fish-
mouths, the O a cavernous word out of the belly
where God is mean and fresh?

A fish?—an angel on the sill?
But what if you accidentally
knock it over? Is that okay with you?—
water slopped from the bowl
through to the sheets, where, deeply, you
are flying in your dreams, the dead
glass flopping around your head?
The whole thing reeks of disappointment.
This line of thinking only gets
you hung up on quiet, peace and quiet.
That's you, resistant to change,
though sometimes you're God and sometimes you're
seafood, fresh out of water, breathing your
big letdown, shocked to see what you've made.

3.

Bagged, fell for it again. You look
to feed off something, and snag, it's eating you.
Say something, won't you? True,
something like utterance has you hooked,
the gasp's old motion was to blame.
Your little ocean heaves forth like a heart
bursting with insight, and while you want,
insensible, to be surprised, you think: flies,
it surely flies, neglecting that it seems,
only seems that I am I,
or that the wings of everything are mid-flight.
Here, after the piercing, comes a still small voice
drying over the rocks where we came up once
before, and found us, and turned back too late.

Velvet

But inside her, there is always velvet,
velvet with its give and yield, the kind you
find at a pet store, a bin full of long
ears and noses busy snuffing up nerves
among the cedar chips and their eyes
opening wide as if rabbits couldn't know
what softness brings, as if they'd never know

the smell of something long stored away now
brought into light, and now too her mother
with a camera pointing at her, red
child on the lap of the Easter rabbit,
softness of the body hiding inside
the costume, eyes glinting from the wide holes
in the mask, not a single sobbing breath

of wind down the trail of mesquite and broom
foot-printing the hills of some rancher's land.
The bird dog lifts his ears to the sound
of velvet, the girl listens to the drawn
cries of a crow, her father walks
with the silence of the shotgun, waiting
for the pointer to find scent, the rabbit
at the end of it blinking, its wide eyes
shrinking from the scuffle of their feet like

velvet settling, laid over lines, drying
across the ceiling of an uncle's garage
where they talk inside the smell of salted
skin. At least three dollars for each good pelt
he says, and they scream like children when,

sleeves rolled over his forearms, he brings
the club down on their heads, saving
their feet for cheap key chains, for luck

that softness doesn't seem to have inside
of cages, chicken wire, tubes of water,
and sometimes boys who try kicking the cage
around to see what happens to velvet
tumbling. And, in the after quiet,
she bites the hands reaching toward her, so they
stone her, they open her belly and pull
some things out, open the pink albino
eye and groan at the fluid inside. Then they
bury the carcass without thinking first
of washing their sticky hands in the sink

before eating dinner, before setting
the table, in the still softness of her
beige room, she sits on the carpet picking
at the velveteen of Bunny's stuffed neck,
the rabbit's eyes dull with scratches, eyes left
behind on her bed at night when she stands
in the hall, hearing her father breathe in his room

in the darkness, on the futon, kicking
off the sheets. Awake from a fluid dream
of a woman's eyes staring from behind
a gag, her white skin settling in fat pools
around her, naked, bald. And a man's
voice said, *this is your rabbit,* so she woke
to this dream inside her, with his teeth wrapped
in her hair, and his hands inside her thighs
where he fingered her coldly. But it has

always been like this—wild, insidious,
and commanding because she gives to it,
fascinated by it and caught by it,
as velvet only listens and is quiet.

The Bells

FLOOD OF '83, CLIFTON-MORENCI, ARIZONA

A rap on the screen, a boy she knows
leaning in the glare at the door,
and she, hearing the sudden plugging
of the church bells, must've looked
startled, for he straightened
and nodded toward the river's ruins
where, he said, they might poke around
on a day like this, this Sunday morning.
His orange cap turns in his methodical hands
as they hike with the din of the bells
down to the old gym and crawl
through one of its busted eyes
into the crypt of the basement damp
where he grips her palm to palm,
and presses her towards a corner
until her mouth dodges his in a daze—
wondering, she can't help it,
if somewhere she has seen this before,
so much vain reaching, almost in passing,
he, laughing, and she too,
laughing, but gauging the tiles back
through the belly of the building
to the stark fact of the outside light,
the bells shifting above floodwater,
Red Cross shovels, sandbags, trucks,
all laboring while the toll from the tower
rises over the wet clay drifts.
She thinks of her father, devoted, among this,
maybe tugging his gloves, maybe worried

about typhoid and tin-dipped water,
or fishing through barrels from helicopters
filled with government cheese and cereal,
how little room there is for awe—
you're so pretty, Jesus so pretty—-
or disillusionment even as it breaks open,
and the fist in her chest stirs
toward the pigeons outside as she feels
his fingers, stiff, in her bra, and a fleck
of sun pierces through the basement panes,
death then beauty. Light, then shape.

Through the Glass

1.

for he maketh me to lie down

Stiff ruffles slide on the pew.
Her legs do not. She kneels to the lace
scraping her ankles and the priest
towers beyond her, slinging a fist
of incense. Smoke sinks down, dims
the burning face of the stained glass.
Voices, as if from a valley,
sounds of an animal dying.

2.

this is the body of christ

Gum balls roll to the ground. She lifts
a rotting board where a mother
scorpion lies down, who is, at last,
supper to the heirs of the old wood.
They writhe at her back and work in,
training to eat the softness
inside. They scurry with the body
to shelter behind a broken bottle.

3.

through the valley of

In the street, a baying of last words
and the hound comes home on three
spirited legs. From his mouth a body of blood,
lungs flat inside his ribs. Her fingers

go to the animal's back where the bone
is undone. In the hall, the rattling
of the glass pane in the door of the gun cabinet,
her father working the key.

4.

through a glass darkly

The great black pot steams the windows
while it waits bubbling for beans.
In her lap, a giant bowl of perfect spotted
pintos, fingers sorting one by one,
buried in the smooth coolness of bean backs.
She peers through the wet eyes
of the ghosts she has drawn on the glass,
singing holy holy this is holy.

These Years, in the Deepest Holes

A summer kite. My father's. It drifts high
over the cemetery gazing down on our little graves.
There is Linda who died in portions. Toes, calves,
thighs, amputated after a black widow bite.
There is Harold, still unmarked. My first suicide.
And someone else, the name escapes me, thrown
vehicle-free on the old intoxicating horseshoe turn.
Now panning back, a man's hand loosens the twine
a little, a little, and a girl picks through the bushes,
flushing cottontails with rocks and sticks,
and there, that is your voice—that is you
mocking epitaphs and plastic flowers. The train snagged
in mesquite, the father and daughter with their hands
at their sides. But where did you come from?
It's bad enough I see you everywhere else.
The man pulls weeds from a plot, his father's,
and tells the girl stories about giant catfish
who lurk these years in the deepest holes of the 'Frisco.
His face labors with words while he yanks,
his gloves stained with the habit of breaking clumps
from roots. You sit nearby and want me to watch you—
that is your way—but I am watching the girl,
listening to her listen. She is fishing
with her father. She remembers a river picnic,
the new bikini she wore, her father saying, come,
let's see how well it fits. Come on. Come here.
When she steps up close, he nods, approves.
She almost walks away but he pulls her
bottom down with a quick peek and laughs.
She toes the ground with past awkwardness,
and looks around for someplace to put it.

You stand behind her. Your arms are crossed,
for it is nothing, gazing down on the greater
scheme of things, most of the time, nothing.
She looks out at the flattened infant graves,
so many, they seem to multiply. They drift
under the earth, small bones. What becomes of them?
They lie in wait. They ascend in time. They return
to devour with their cries for attention.

Everything Goes Down a Changeling

A great cloud of tiny insects—ingenious,
the summer light sifted through all those wings
like that, like a thought shifting
over a bog veined in bright water.
The air was coming down
with an imminent rain—I could feel it.
And you were there, shaking your head,
smiling at the camera though I felt slighted.
Everything goes down a changeling, you said.
You've got to have it how you can.
So it was hopeless already when I noticed
that my legs were running
with blood, with mosquitoes thickly drowning,
when you turned from me saying,
well, it's what you wanted.

Darkling

It happened gradually. My hands, always behind me, sore
from picking at ropes, went first.
They began to feel light and hollow, though something prickled
beneath the skin. My fingers closed and fused,
my arms grew narrow and long
until they were twice the length of my body.
Then, my heart. It raced ahead of me
and tried to thrash its way out—
philomel, philomel—-
I listened, afraid to speak.
I thought the hush could do me no harm.
But in silence my tongue was severed.
I'd watched it writhe on the ground in front of me, murmuring,
dividing, becoming forked before it slithered off.
When feathers finally appeared in patches, I saw
that you can live, mute and still, with a sharp desire
for your father's country, which is power.
Or you deny your name until it feels like strength,
and give away all but your scarlet hair,
for it might bring recognition
when you feel murderous, waiting, impatient to do nothing,
turning away from a spindly light that burns your eyes.
You sleep all day, wake fitfully in the evening,
dream of a lover as gentle as your father.
Out of any long-chosen habit you will be transformed
if you are living in want.
He will leave again, and he will return, of course he will.
He will leave, brandishing his coiled weapon
that makes you convulse with longing
to sing.

That He Will Land and Find His Feet

FRANKENSTEIN'S CASTLE, CLIFTON, ARIZONA

1.

She had seen a boy once who knew everything
(dare me?) step too far crossing the ties
of the black train bridge where the lines of smooth steel
lay ahead and ahead, tracks of the copper Southern Pacific
placed like teeth, three feet apart—
he had stepped, slipped through fifty feet of air,
smacked the sliver of green river water and rocks below.
At night, every night smothered beneath him,
she sees him rise up and walk away
as if over the gleam of water, floating.

2.

How his feet must feel,
bare and shadowed,
thinking it will
not pass, time
will not pass; how
he dares to close his eyes
pillowed by that
eyelid-black
in a quaking sky.
A position:
poised like a fragment
of moon hung out, not
an ornament, not to dry,
but to mend
that space
between hopeless

and landing,
between the gray
of day and—is it
night yet? No,
there! Like a flashlight
dropping
he has jumped, a wink,
a romantic glint
of white, with one
foot making two
things sure—
that he will land
and find his feet
and body submerged.

The Spirit that Appears When You Call

What are you doing in the house of my sleep with your merciless
goods and your gravity?

I crept to the shed and crouched in darkness
where the outside light cut into the dust, the motes
I stirred up floating into view, falling, rising up again.
I took them into my lungs. I sat on an anvil
beneath the workbench in the good scent
of chicken feed and straw, seeing the bear traps
on the wall and the meat hook gingerly tucked
into a fish head the size of my own. Because no place
I've known is still and small as this one,
in wind and after fire I was not afraid.

What is it now—the assiduous virus? The oblivious host of things
    revered?

My ears ached. I hid them with my hands,
but the infection was deafening, so I clutched my head
and walked around for days in silence, watching clothes flap
on the line without a sound. Wind chimes were mute.
A pot boiled over, forgetting, my hand burned
in the hush. Poultices of hot salt, teaspoons of olive oil
warmed on the heater, until the first sound—a voice—
came out of the muffle, tremulous, although
I could hear him: his face turned away,
but his hands, full of life, animated with talking.

It is always about you, your persistence, your terrible departure
with your hobo stick and your witchcraft books.

In one of the books, a spell to summon a demon
from the asylum of chalk on the bedroom floor.
Incense must burn at each point of the perfect star
drawn in a perfect pentagon, and the spirit that appears
when you call will be your slave. In another book,
notes from an alchemist's journal tell of a miniature garden
inside a jar where for 24 hours a tiny man and woman
live in paradise. The basic ingredient, animal tincture,
was nowhere explained, though I searched glossaries
and *National Geographic,* wanting a blueprint for birth.

You come with your censors, you come with your talismans, your indigo
rabbit, your inkblot paintings, your crucifix that glows in the dark.

The poems were a secret. I wrote about love and rain,
and the fire in my mind, and roses, velvet roses.
I wrote fast. I memorized. I ran rhymes through my head
scrub-brushing the toilet and sitting through dinner.
Alone in the laundry room that smelled of bleach
and metallic water, I wrote. I listened to the white witch
purr about dreams and madness over and over
on my eight-track stereo, and I heard rumors in the house
that someday soon I'd be found out. On the way to school
I burned what I wrote and kept the visions to myself.

There were fires behind you, sermons, candles, brimstone, light,
Lucifer christened in the rattle of tongues and a tambourine—

From the beginning I felt for Eve, who before anyone, knew loss.
Before poor Cain, before the blood-red clusters of the tree,
there was Adam. Adam's Eden, Adam's animals, Adam's rib.
And she was a wisp of hair. When the serpent called to her,
she was surprised. She might have said: Me?
Are you talking to me? Don't you want to talk to my husband?

She was surprised, and unafraid, when at last there came a chance
for something more, some subtle turn of mind, her own mind,
coming to grips with the nagging emptiness and boredom, which now
she thought were on the eve of leaving her, with a single bite.

You doubted. No one could explain the ruins poised just above
the mine on the horizon. You crossed the tailings dam
night by night, white lime on your lashes, you in doubt.

There were floods and famines, browns and whites,
miners and the company, tenants in The Hole and residents
of Jackrabbit Flats, water for drinking and water, sulfate blue,
welling up the slag banks of Chase Creek. There were mornings
of clarity and mornings to smelt, days for the swing-shift, days
off for church, priests for burial, reverends in tents. There were
wives and whores, part-timers and company men, hours
for union workers, salaries for supervisors, effigies burned past town
and scabs bashed at the gates. There were guitar assemblies, tear gas
set by the national guard, curfews, contracts, copper prayers, the gods.

What of the seizures? What of lightness and heaviness, the task
of figuring just where you'd get to?

When the water spilled over the wall, I was there,
at the riverside, looking into the swollen waves,
the dog in my arms, people in front of me crowding to watch
a yellow crane clear driftwood, uprooted willows, a white
refrigerator dammed against the bridge. Sirens wailed
over the rising river and we raced the flood to the outskirts,
trapped, hours later, high up on the surrounding red hills,
pointing to rooftops of three-story buildings: all we could see.
We waited through the night, the rain
pouring down over the blackout like a shroud.

Was it you that night, you in astonishment, running
through the streets in your socks, hearing the sound of a head
strike the pavement like a bottle?

After the funeral, cousins showed up to the house
with a trumpet, an accordion, a few guitars, and we sat
at night in cheap lawn chairs around the backyard
singing sad songs in Spanish, eating and drinking,
while the men smoked cigars and drifted around the grill
that hissed with beef skirts and green chilies. I can still
hear them, they come back, the men with their stories,
when Johnny got pissed, Cabron! Como chingas!
the women sighing, his heart, his heart, the cousins
in gold and black sombreros, Y volver, volver, volver—

you wanted to scream
to get just get the hell
to cut to scrawl all over all my life the goddamn crybaby
you crybaby you why can't you
like a normal person
Jesus what the fuck is
you freak what is your problem
why can't you just
cry

That was how he died, how he died inside
when we called him garbage can man, when we
laughed at his perm-rolled hair, his old white truck,
his greasy egg-yolk sandwiches. He died inside
when he drank, when he tried to smoke when
everybody else smoked. He died inside when we'd spy him
getting high on the stoop with a sawed-off shotgun at his feet
and a picture of a boy he knew. He died inside

the littered cab of his primer-dappled old truck,
chest gaping, eyes gaping, when the cavity at last came out.

You were digging holes in the backyard corner, tearing your nails
and pulling up stones. You talked to yourself, you sought
a way in, I could hardly make out what you said.

They prayed over me at the front of the church, hands
on my shoulders, arms up to the heavens, *sweet lord,*
they prayed, *let this child receive the blessing of tongues.* I knelt
lord, sucking air, *thy innocent child* rocking like a windfall,
she comes before thee now, beneath the preacher's palm, *please hear,*
the sweat on my forehead, *lord jesus answer our prayers,* praying that God
wouldn't appear to strike me down *in the name of the Holy Spirit*
for lack of faith, *for she has given her heart to you,* for the time
I'd struck my brother, for parleying with the devil, *for her brothers
and sisters ask,* for shame, *that you let this child speak.*

You were bored. You dropped huge rocks into the river pools
and your reflection shuddered like your shouts on the cliffs,
summoning back the shock of what you are.

My brother was fearless. He'd go tearing down the trail
in the empty lot behind our house, gaining speed
on his motocross bike, hit the ramp, lift the front wheel,
and fly. He flew over garbage cans. He flew over a stack
of milk crates. It's all in the ramp, he'd say. We found
an old door in the lot and propped it up on boulders,
piling dirt beneath it. I'd lie down in front of our ramp,
looking up at the sky, hearing his tires barrel down the path,
and I'd wait for the familiar groan and yield of the door,
when my brother, with an art I worshipped, flew over me.

You tore into the house, up the stairs and into the hall, singing
bloody bloody bones, can you hear me?

Abandoned by her lover after a violent fight,
a dark-haired woman dressed all in white veils gives birth
to a bastard by the river. In rage and sorrow she shines,
she burns in the moonlight, holding the child, holding it
under water till its lungs are filled. She wanders,
I have seen her, she takes my breath away, la llorona,
creeping through mesquite in the canyons, looking for the spirit
of her newborn baby in the faces of those who stray too late
at night. I've seen her eyes glitter like stars between branches,
and she considered me, she considered taking me.

You set fire to the curtains, fire to the doors, in the inconsequential
days of belief. Something divine. You would have burned
down the house in my sleep.

In the photograph a blizzard takes over, veiling all but a few
dark shapes in the background, a road sign, maybe. A highway.
The sun behind her is a small, powdery eye. It sees the back
of her yellow coat, her hood pulled up around her head,
her ankles exposed. And still, who would have thought,
some accident has frozen the sun. It longs
after the woman turned away, facing me. Her arms flail, her scarf
flutters at her chin, her chin is curved like mine. Her eyes,
another accident, dark, like mine. One more frame and she will fall.
Her body aches with it, eternity, equilibrium, a call for help.

The old iron furnace, its forging, its forgery, was it for this,
is it for this, that you are leaving, that you
have never left off?

I crept into the shed and crouched on an anvil.
Above me the hook swayed gently on the end
of its chain, in and out of the piercing light, the fish head
suspended face down as if intent on listening
to the doves' wings scuttling and rasping outside
against the roof, their cries all at once high, terrified
and trapped, countless and identical, like the motes
and the down drifting from the sky into the restless dust
of the shed. Feathers, like embers, like a window of stars,
fell into view, glimmered with promise, dissolved.

TWO

Old gods are terrible to look at when

They weep, all bloated like spoiled fish.

One wonders if they ever understand

That they have caused their own grief. When the seventh day

Came, the flood subsided from its slaughter

Like hair drawn slowly back

from a tormented face.

—Gilgamesh

The Walk Like Old Habits

It seems unlikely, how the city repeats itself
without describing your life. Peeling billboards,
chinks in the walls. Girls on the corner make signs
to one another in the dust, balconies turn
from the beggars rearing up like mannequins
and you think truth is there, however unintelligible.
But it does not wake you to street names you imagine
said something adequate in the beginning, if ever
one street was not like the next, if ever this place
was not like Venice, not like Beijing, but itself
the first lone thing under the sun. Like the garden
before it was *their* garden: the sun before ritual,
before gods, sprouting from stones and fountains, mad, mad,
before all things unremarkable, as winter, as excrement.
Nor does the sudden maze of bicycles and storefronts
bring a word to mind, nothing more than concrete,
brick, glass, motion, all useless, really, though you
come across a woman who sorts through a box
of white fruit, her face pocked with scars
you might recognize should the moon appear full
to announce a point of origin or pleasure that is free
of mooning on every waterway you see. If only
love were free of spit and image, and image—interrupted
by the bells, bells, bells calling from towers
in churchyards where lie the beloved in crates—were
free of rivals. Laughter erupts from a place, many,
beyond the canals, the canals below chimneys
and cemeteries and temple steps, the steps
where old men watch boys mock them, now limping,
now drooling, now trying on an old man's palsy
leafing through a book: licks a deliberating finger,

turns to the pages like the living turn to bread.
The corpses. The guillotines reminiscent of lab rats
stand in for revolution in the square, the emperor
moves through the crowd like a crisis coming
to a head. Heads and more heads in the streets,
this street where you open your eyes and find, isn't it
strange, that you do not grieve the bare infant
you gather to yourself from the walk like old habits
reminding you that some things are new, this body
who wakes you, new hands, new eyes. So little
do you know yourself and the light you would make
even here, to the quick, embracing small things
that grasp you—it's me, it's me—that you
look up for the grounds of your blessings.

Where the Bodies, Half-Dressed, in Pieces

FOR CARMEN RIOS, FLOOD VICTIM, DEL RIO, TEXAS, AUGUST 22, 1998

What blessings are left to them? They heap belongings
on the walk. Stones washed from their walls
lie about like teeth, one ache next to another.
Nature remains. A sodden box of photos, a wet TV.
A pile of Christmas ornaments winks
in the sun, so there is miracle. They find
new mosquitoes in toilets. In the kitchens, mold
creeps over the windows, in the bedrooms, a goat's
carcass, a bag of trash, a used diaper,
a tree. They find they can put their hands
through walls. Of clay. So there is also
belief. Had belief come sooner, had a forecast
arrived—*listen, it's rain—the drought
is over—the flatlands are running over*—but all
is quiet. Not yet a downpour, patient
at doors, not the emergency broadcast system
streaming across every screen. Not sirens,
thunder, screams, houses shuddering,
giving way below those crouching
on their rooftops. Not yet. First came
coincidence, a twist of fate, a man who towed
his motorboat to the nearby lake, trapped mid-storm
outside his neighborhood. Countless he rescued.
A woman hugging a rushing bush, brothers
perched on a truck, the old man who sells
melons all summer: where was he but among
the saved? So there are also numbers.
When the deluge arrived, I felt
eternity. I left my house. I took up
my cane and walked around in the dark, flicking

switches, banging into things, fighting, until I found
the door. I was up to my neck, swirling.
When it was time, water swallowed me too, down
in a cold flash to the streets where the hill
ends, where the bodies, half-dressed, in pieces,
are torn away from dreams. At Devil's Bend, bodies
collected with trees and refrigerators. The water
receded. The crane dug up hundreds rotting
off the bone, nine of whom were identified
as citizens. I am with them and their families
in the paper below the mayor's address. The rest
were mejicanos, so of course there is also home.
In the funeral home where my daughter didn't find me,
there was a body, stripped of all but a ring
that resembled my own, but again, it was not mine,
so for a time there was also hope.

Paraffin Days

1.

She prays her rosary each night twice, she
keeps track of each plastic bead, she prays
as beads slip past *our father,* past the maze
of faltering sons who visit because they see
themselves someday in beds like these. Beds she's
wet. And she's prayed her rosary away
from mourning, beads of plastic, legs of clay—
sshh. Listen: living seems connected (she
asks *who has brought this rosy potpourri*)
to voices, her voice spilling over tiles
and streets, bedroom thresholds, puddles lined
with mud: she dips child's hands into this, tells
herself the story of paraffin days:
a house, a husband, children, someday.

2.

And living seems like days collected, my
brass bowl of petals, my own voice in words
across the page—yet that's gone too—I've heard
its metal gleam slip soft to silence, and I
remember this: a silver crucifix,
a pendant lost to the sea sinking that way—
it's not so difficult, is it, to say
that out there somewhere, settled in the sand, it is
still on fire, exists like a god who listens
but cannot answer except in sounds
of water, in sounds of salt crusting the rocks,
where life at once dragged up and chose its end,
its shape: the fire in the cells vivid
as wishes, as things engraved in stone, as luck.

3.

This wick, lit from flames before it,
sways in the continuity of want.
As wish breeds wish and the room fills with light,
so I take hold: these days, inherently,
are mine. I kneel and watch the shadows cross
a letter someone's left to the saints. The writing
aches among the candles, desire flitting
from flame to flame, furious to realize
its transience, transcending my own
doubts. I remember my loves-me petals
all let loose on the wind, the crowned
stems left empty, but the making, hopeful.
The act itself denies any last convictions,
makes light of constellations.

"That Cried to the Whole City 'Sleep no More'"

Last night the bulb in the kitchen went without
warning, the third this week. I woke with you
sometime early and walked through the park
before the sun came up, or sometime later when
she, when he, still lay sleeping with the baby,
when we were walking the house in socks
so as not to wake, I woke, and we were waking
with loathing, and with coffee and cigarettes
we cleaned up the refuse of last night's routine,
and made breakfast of a burning bagel, or
shuffled through documents and newspaper,
or poured water on the desiccated plants before
feeding the hungry from a cat-food can before hitting
the snooze, before leaving him in bed
to sleep it off, or stepping with a headache
into the driveway in need of paving, and before walking
as always to the office we ran late after sex, thought
I wish I could get that song out of my head,
and raced the trash to the curb before the truck arrived,
or were on the truck since five this morning
with the stench of flesh and rot, with the others
who are just as good with a hammer
as you are, but not as smart. And we cursed work
and the week, for it is only Tuesday, only Tuesday,
when I woke, flicked a switch: Christ what now?—
and remember, the bulb. I wonder
what became of the little guarantee in the box,
white light, ordinary luster, 50 percent longer life—
haven't I witnessed softness, preservation, ease,
gone with a flicker of fire and smoke, in what,
do you know? The room is dark but for the set:

the plane, the tower, combustion,
one hundred and forty-five thousand tons of debris,
the firemen tapping the earth for a voice,
last minute calls from a brand-new cell—
I had been reading Wordsworth
that morning of all things
who was pleading for a common language,
something repetitious and full of feeling
that might finally lead us to permanence,
to the study of truth. But the truth is,
when it happened, I was on the phone
telling a friend about some old love
who has made me ill, who stays like the image
of blood, ciphered and shelved, just for the sake
of something to do. Last minute calls
from a brand new cell—five thousand fold—
something repetitious—how many planes?
How many did you hear? What is there
to do but return to the habit
of combat and sit with the dead and wonder,
if I had not been hit this way, over
and again, if not for this edifice of graves,
this apex of things in a complex
of things I have never lived without,
and without bodies, portions laid out
in the light for the living who are
walking the concrete waste, and if not
for windows, opening onto the slumbering
city morning, how could I know dominion
and prayer, reverting and enduring
as it was meant for me in the beginning?
How could I know? Tell me
For I am sick with knowing.

Del Rio

———

In her yard a woman fans herself, weighing
the drought against roses she planted
when her daughter left home. She knows this year
honeysuckle and bougainvillea prove
well enough. Let them bloom and make the house
new. Let them weigh down their trellises
with climbing. With what guilt
should she suffer the roses, what
heart? She knows there will be
pictures to take of the new
scrap-wood deck. She will send photos once
the banana plants have overshadowed even
the wind in the garbage, even the work
left behind again by the men for the sake
of a job that came up. Thank God. First
things first: the overgrown lawn. She works.
It is the work of lifting up grievances. It is heavy,
this contract, this handful of terrors, each a small
marvel of appetite, each working like saints
to weary her reach. Let them. Her daughter
will come home. She won't recognize it.

———

Each time I go back
a new dog growls at the gate.
What happened to the last one, I ask.
That one? That one has been gone for a long time.

———

The dogs got hold of the mango plant last night.
Out the door, the porch, towards the driveway gate,
but today, before leaving the house, we were stopped
by the sapling, my mango. I come to this as I come
to most misgivings: you moon, look sleepy, look held
from your metronome this morning. You look disappointed
with this exhausting land of deer standing in the highway.
Didn't I drive all night with the plant on the dash?
All night the bugs, the wet, had slapped the glass,
a one-sided conversation on drowning. I talked to myself
for hours, watching road signs, and the leaves warbled gladly.
There are starting places that prove impossible.
My mother and I sweep up stems and soil.
There are failures that need not be erected.

———

The fruit-stand leans on the corner, warm with apples,
heady with oregano. We buy limes for our soup and stop
by the factory where tortillas sweat in their plastic
on the shelves. Our shoes smear soft tracks through the flour
on the floor as we leave and the old man parked

on Bean Street knows from our dusty coins where we
have just been. He was parked there yesterday, too,
selling melons from the back of his truck. Three dollars, two
for the little ones, which are less sweet and have too many seeds.
We taste the sandía he cuts open, shake off our wet hands.

Behind the truck, a low creek runs through the canna lilies,
pampas grass, great-leaved elephant ears crowded by the water.
Two children wade in their underwear. They chase crayfish

from the moss—fork them, and toss them in bait buckets—
unafraid, even as I fear for them, taking them in my hands.

———

Meanness: only the first language without firsthand
knowledge of the second, only the voicelessness
of the river building sadness inside her
that she might come to match the inaccessible hush
of the current sweeping in to sweep her within it.

———

They are building a prison down the block.
This came to pass without warning.
The little house on the lot of trees, the trailer
next door, the nectarines and ragweed summers
won't sell. They make sacrifices,
they are resourceful. They bring a truckload of mesquite
from the river and nail a cardboard sign to the fence.
The details—firewood, five and ten dollars a bundle—
don't tell you how it burns, staunch and slow with us,
huddled by the stove, my brother and I,
remembering.
        Remember? Eerie, that meadow
on the reservation, how it glittered like a parking lot,
all that obsidian, shit loads of it, everywhere,
every shard, smaller than a fingernail, like this,
clear as smoked glass and *shining* till you got up close
and found that what you have there in your palm
is just like sawdust, remnants of some guy's expertise,
some long-ago guy sitting right there on the ground,
carving arrowheads. Once you've picked up a few
that have failed, once you realize they all look pretty much

the same, you know how careful he was, that guy.
You know what he was thinking, you've felt that way,
working over some small point before bed. You think
if you can get it right, exactly, this thing will fly
right to the heart, and there will be feasting, dancing,
days of ease, time to hang around the house
watching movies with your wife, and your kids—
they want to go swimming? It is payday, man. It's the weekend.
Everybody, I mean everybody, is going swimming.

———

When was the last time you went down
to the river with your brother, cousins, the babies
squirming to get down from your arms, the back
of the truck loaded with grocery bags
full of corn chips, suntan lotion, towels,
warm coke, and you in cut-offs and sunglasses,
smothered in bug repellant, hunting
for driftwood to burn on the fire? Let's go
down to the river, sit on the sand, blast
the car stereo till we burn the old
battery. We'll load up the ice chest
with cheap meat, take the babies
into the shallows and show them minnows,
we'll let them run naked, they love
to be naked, Mami scolding for leaving
the diaper bag behind. Marranos! Behind
us the sun drifts down in the usual
way. Richard tells stories of his days
as a prison guard, the last supper
this guy painted, the guy who learned
English reading auto manuals, who ran
down three teens on a drunken binge, who

spent all day with his rosary praying
for his brothers who deserve a better life.
How warm it is today. How late when the beer
runs low and the babies have lost their good
shoes, too, just as they did the last time.

————

My mother and grandmother raking the backyard,
sipping water, they gossip. They tell
me about the kid two blocks
from Garza's, you know Garza's, well this kid
was a sniffer, paint, glue, you name
it, and he was already kind of
messed up in the head, and one night,
just like that, stabbed and raped
his mama. Just like that.

————

And this detail I can fondle
like a knot—one limp knot
untying itself as my uncle drops a skewer
in the dirt, bends over his loose shoe
and beside the skewer, by chance,
a dandelion he plucks up from the heat
waving around the grill. Without words
we are shy. He hands me his prize, grins,
prods the ribs with the skewer he wipes on his jeans.
Of course I hope, from one side
of the country between, that I am
laughable, longing,
needless as it is—not futile, but absurd—
to hesitate
as a breeze takes the seeds for root elsewhere.

———

Whose side are you on, anyway?

So this wetback walks into a bar
with this big parrot on his shoulder, and the bartender says,
Hey that's pretty nice-looking, where'd you get that?
And the parrot says, Oh down in Mexico.
They've got a lot of them there.

———

I amuse him. What else, then? he asks
for my sake in English. His tongs
hover above the aluminum trays
covered in pink and yellow sugar. Pan dulce,
empanaditas filled with pineapple
or pumpkin, green and red
shortbread galletas, and these
I love, pig-shaped breads, ginger-scented,
whose name varies from place to place.
Cochitos, I say, holding up three
fingers, pressing the glass. The man
smiles wider, enunciating. Marranitos.
I hand him two dollars,
but he waves me away, and I step out
of the sweetness of the bakery into the warmth
of sunset, the silence of Sunday,
with tomorrow's breakfast wrapped in paper
like a gift. After evening mass
the man inside scoops the morning's
left-over menudo into paper cups
for the night's winos, and already a woman
sits fanning on the floor boards, waiting

44

with flies for nothing she can name. Corazón,
she says to me, and she waves
at the air, and I nod, it is all I can do,
for I am allowed. I am grateful too.
I almost know what she means.

Where it Goes

3/22/00
10:35:13 AM
Eastern Standard Time

Chris got a job offer he's thinking he'll take.
He would be gone a week or two at a time
but we'd get 500 dollars a week,
1,000 every two. He wouldn't drive,
meals and hotel are covered, it sounds good
even if its time on the road. You cousin joe got offered
one too but the thing is I was telling your mom,
he has a habit (and you know what I mean)
he can't travel with. He can bearly get home
for lunch before puking. Oh and they would be
setting up plumbing displays for all the McCoys
in texas. They had another job but thier boss already
bid. Rumor is the plumbing co. will file bankrupsee
so i told chris we take care of ourselves first, boy.

3/23/00
10:16:22 AM
Eastern Standard Time

Everyone is doing good here.
But I wanted to share with you what i saw on tv.
First and for most you are

not yet doomed to walk the earth
with out kids. the latest trend is having kids
at an older age. maddona is pregnant with

47

her second at the age of 42. susan sarandes
had one at 45. then there's kathy lee grifford.
the names might not be spelled right and

i'm feeding baby carla so take pity.
your mom is painting the trim around the house.
Well dan is doing the painting actually.

No more about that job. Chris gets
all excited and then
you never hear anything else about it.

3/25/00
7:16:23 PM
Eastern Standard Time

Your mom caught a bird in the house
last night after me and Chris left.
There was a wedding dinner so I put
on a spagetti strap dress and washed
my hair but your mom said
she had the perfect out fit for me and she
takes me in her room fixes
my hair and my makeup saying she
hadn't done this since you were
little. then we were off and we ate
and sat around laughing
at people. They played Spanish
music and we danced next to this chick
wearing black spandex which would've been
cute except she was HUGE and her ass
hung out flopping under her shirt. But she could dance.

She got out there swinging that thing, her butt
doing this wave/ripple affect. There was a cousin
of ya'lls named jesus who's supposed
to be a child malester. I would have never
noticed, but chris said watch
who the fucker's looking at and darned if
he wasn't watching the little girls
and i felt my stomach turn. All of a sudden
he came to the house today with Mario
and they were teasing the bird. I tried
to keep alisa out of sight. I don't care
how big chris is, once something
happens it will bring me no pleasure
seeing the guy punished.
It won't change what's happened.

3/27/00
11:21:30 AM
Eastern Daylight Time

I was happy to get your letter. I had a rough day.
My step-mom had a breakdown and is in a hospitol.
I don't understand all the why's of it. She has paranoia
scetsafrinia. (and i know that is spelled totally
wrong). I don't blame myself I just didn't see it coming.

When the rest of the family hated her I was there
because they didn't understand her the way I did.
It sounds crazy but even before this happened,
she would dream things that would come true.
Chris knows even if he thinks she's always been crazy.

A couple a months ago, while I was still pregnant

she had a miscarrige and she turned to her religion
stronger than ever. My dad said sunday she left for church
at 7 am and still wasn't home at 11 pm! It turns out
she had been in a different state of mind since last monday.

And come to find out she went to church and told everybody
that Jesus was coming. They kicked her out so she went
door to door. I was told she was dangerous. She thought
my dad was satan and she attacked him at the hospital
because he was stopping her from what God told her to do.

She hadn't slept in three days. I am still lost.
I don't understand why her religion?
I have a friend and she has M.S. and she is gorgeous
And in years to come her body will shrivel up
And your grandma and her fear of storms.
I don't understand why our weakness?

    3/29/00
    10:12:37 AM
    Eastern Standard Time

They hired someone at your moms office
so your mom isn't swamped and i helped word
her letter to the morgage co. for an extention
because they said she wasn't specific
enough so i sounded like dan is on
his death bed and the house completely
trashed since the flood. well, it's kinda true.

3/30/00
5:09:58 PM
Eastern Standard Time

Chris and dan are off today. they told the boss
they didn't want to work for him. I heard dan telling chris

what he told him and that about summed it up.
How are you doing? hows the weather? Did the rain stop?

The girls are doing fine. lately Alisa has a bad attitude
and carla is spoiled rotten. Not to mention huge.

Alisa is still working on the potty thing
but its better. When she misses she likes to say DANG.

i was up late talking to my dad. he was upset over some thing
my step mom did. and it shocked me the way he was talking.

Its been a wierd week already. The dog we got named blue
ran away the same day we got him. Nobody knew.

but your mom is doing ok. dan is good.
chris is fine even though he's mad at your dad.

your dads letters chris sends to him keep coming
back like they changed the address or something.

```
3/30/00
6:49:29 PM
Eastern Standard Time
```

```
From: MAILER-DAEMON@cs.com
Destination error message general translation: the
following address had permanent fatal errors: tran-
script of session follows: reason message not deliv-
ered line beginning "<<<" describes specific failure
to connect: message ID <32.39fe585.267a8e6> content-
transfer-encoding: Host Unknown
```

```
4/3/00
5:26:56 PM
Eastern Daylight Time
```

Well it is official.
The guys no longer work for Rick.
Dan already designed a bussiness card and they are thinking about
flyers
and there is this guy who works for a company
in mexico who said he can do it there 8 cards for .25 cents.
So we shall see.
They talked to the man that inspects their work and he knows
they will pay someone to get permits for the jobs, so he won't
bother them he even gave a list of people to use.
Thats good.
The only thing is the obvious.
When you have your own co. you can't blow off work all day.

4/4/00
11:43:15 AM
Eastern Daylight Time

My step-mom is better from what they say.
She went from red (suicidal watch) to green (she can
use the bathroom by herself and walk around).
She is very Mexican and uses herbs so my dad said
the drugs give her problems. She hit the I Hate You
For Putting Me Here stage but my dad is Hanging In There

The flood is still here. I don't think it will ever be
totally cleaned up. Partly because the city
has already forgot but partly I think to remember.
I can't explain how it was.
I've seen blizzards and tornadoes but this
has its own place in natural disaster.

The guys and their co. are doing ok.
It would seem Eric their ex-boss left town as of
yesterday! So everyone is looking for him including
us. He needs to fill out employment papers for the food
stamp office for me and chris. So we ended
up fighting last night over a stupid
inventory printing. The printer was not printing (because it is
broken).
but I need to clean house so my hubby doesn't have
a cow in my livingroom. Be glad you don't have
one. never marry ok. Live ins are all
right but when you marry all that charm
and flattery fades away.
Where everything goes I have no clue.

Their Lives and Shadows

Again with the camcorder. Somebody makes
a gift of stolen property and suddenly
we're watching ourselves from my brother's angle
since he knows how to make it work:
the parakeet shivers in his bamboo cage,
my brother's wife pulls her hair
into a rubber band and scolds the baby
eating popcorn from her lap, in loving memory
a two-foot crucifix nailed to the turquoise wall:

Carla, look over here, that's right, smile.
God girl, you got some big lips. You need
to give your tía some of those lips—
she's been checking out pictures of that carp
we caught when we were kids and all week
she's been wishing for a mouth like that.

The same nose too small on his face,
the same thick bottom lip. He pruned
the fruit trees in the same shirt he wore
yesterday. He set fire to the branches
and they singe the sky between us, the sparks
waking like identical lives of more
and more stars. He sits in a fold-up chair
through the night, his bourbon, companion:

You don't remember that night? Man how could you
forget we were freezing our cojones at the reservoir,
it was just this skinny little moon and the lake
was black, black. I mean we had ten poles
cast every which way and because the rain
was clinging to the lines we could just make them out,

like webs in the headlights of the truck.
Tudy kept saying they're biting bro,
that's why they're vibrating like that, it'll work,
and Richard's going you're full of shit you drive
a truck all weekend, that's algae, weeds.

Weeds, lime-green water, four hundred feet
below our bare legs the silt skates over
the lake bottom, lurking below us.
Something great and bright lies deep looking up,
flashes through the murk too quick for sight,
and he swims in pursuit. I tread near shore
where dead fish quiver with the scuttle and pick
of crayfish, small hearts, small black eyes,
shadows their lives and shadows out far, the buoy
and my brother, faces brooding on the surface.

Well, Tudy lights match after match, he chews
on the end of a joint, tight as a toothpick
between his wide lips, and all he can get
is this lank wet smoke, and it reeks like a carcass.
Oyes, not even weeds he says inhaling.
So we reel in the lines, toss everything
into the pickup, and pile into the cab to sleep.

Sleep for him like a phantom limb
even before the cocaine days. Nothing so pure
as whiteness searing into the daily brown tunnels:
and you dig and you dig until the day the guy
you worked with for years loses an arm
to a bulldozer. *Time to quit* before you
break down in front of those before you,
your father, Carlos, your father's father, Juan,
their aluminum lunchboxes, their steel-toed boots,

their malachite gifts, azurite, cuprite, fool's gold,
at time, dear pilferage, the cost of a job.

In the morning we see that we forgot one,
the old yellow pole we stole with the busted reel.
Richard pulls on the line, it's stuck,
and yeah, we should just knife it,
but we're already wet, we smell like seafood,
we're in trouble when we get home no matter what,
so Tudy goes after the hook, and he pulls,
and Richard wraps an unbelievable amount
of fishing string around his hand and elbow,
and there they are, our tíos, the oldest
and the youngest brother swearing what if
it's a fucking corpse, man, what then?——-

Night, gang fight: we could just make them
out, two boys, brothers with shotguns
weaving down Shannon Hill and across
the railroad ties of the Black Bridge, barrels
and cowboy hats cocked to the sky.
We hide behind a parked car.
Out of the quiet neighborhoods the cholos
arrive with chains and switchblades, following,
whistling to one another in the streets, calling
from the dark: We want to talk to you: Yeah?
Then come out here you pussies, the brothers say.
Another whistle. You imitate the call—what
the hell are you doing, I whisper—and one sets
off in our direction, staring through the crosshairs.

—while you and me stand around cold as death,
shaking, rubbing our hands for warmth,
thinking mama's going to kill her brothers

for keeping us out here all night,
and all at once, this gigantic matalote the size
of Tudy's leg, not fighting, not caring, shores up,
and it's shining. It shines with the heaviness
of the sun on all those scales, heavier than life.

They beat the crap out of you and left you
for dead. I didn't ask who. You slept in fits
on my couch, three days in a worn
McDonald's uniform, your feet dangling
over the end, you slept. I came home
to find you spooning chili into your mouth
from a can one day: *Yeah, it tasted like*
dog food. No—you remember those two pit bulls
we had, how they used to chew through
coffee cans and chains, their mouths all
lacerated and shit, their gums infected?
That's how it tasted. Like metal, like blood.

Inscribed on back: Mama and Tudy with the big fish.
Beside them a bucket and a tiny white stove.
He stoops and still a rafter dents his afro.
Beneath the sleeves of a small jacket, needle tracks,
tattoos, and below the cuffs, his great hands
in the red gills. He looks for all the world
as if the catch, life-sized, length of his leg,
is of no great concern. He raises an eyebrow,
his eyes stare out at the camera into the face,
yours, taking the picture. At his wake, the resemblance
no one could help pointing out. *They beat him*
to a pulp, left him for dead. Yes, beyond recognition.
And he dares us to make something of it.

Let Us Rest

Weekends, only, to pity
my father. What he couldn't face—
what hurt him were the socks that fell
from the hamper in knots,
the dish he would wash, the one dish
and fork left to dry on the counter.
Accumulating dust, this alone.
As always, he is at the sink now, rinsing
with slow worried hands, he is tying
the trash bag, shoulders and back, repenting,
his neck, his arms, bent in private alarm:
Do you see? It is painfully clear,
he is caught in the task, unaware, not quite,
of how empty it is, of how much he spirits away
now that—if you could see him you'd know this—
he is sleeping alone. It is the story of my life,
how it starts. To begin with, an offering:
another clean plate, and here are your socks,
your sheets, and here, let me,
the pleasure is mine, I imagine,
and the glass always full, and I am sure
this once and for all that sleep will come,
for here it is, the end of another long week.
Let us rest.
I mean no disservice, let me, let us,
get out of my sight, unsightly as we are,
my father, my mother too, here, like addiction,
my addiction, and the intoxicating
talismans against it.

What We Give

GLEN, WE DAREN'T GO A-HUNTING

Through the turnstile past the sign that says this way
to Mexico, through the taxi drivers and the vendors' calls
to buy, come buy, this way, one hundred percent off
for you today güeritas, what you are looking for,
I have it, magic, whatever you want, if you speak English
to me for one minute—momentito—what you want,
chess sets? blankets? This man here will carve
your boyfriend's name into a small brass ring,
and for you the women in doorways hold up
their hands, muttering in Spanish, a little
cooperation, please. The tethered children squat
nearby, siblings push bracelets and boxes
of colorful gum in the road, eddying, jostling,
while we press on towards el centro but stop
a boy with a cart of paletas to buy dos de arroz,
cold, pink, sweet, gracias, for it is muggy
in the crowd and the sidewalks reek of sewer and sweat
while we walk to Maricela's house, a ways to go yet,

swatting mosquitoes that circle our ankles
even inside the pharmacy where we stand
in line at the counter and overhear a conversation
between the cashier and a girl who holds
an empty plastic jug in one hand and sways
from foot to bare foot. Come on, she says,
I know you have some, and the cashier smiles,
saying, no mija, really we have no running water here,
and the girl shifts in her purple dress, twirls
softly, lands by the bottled water in the sweltering

61

cooler and begins to trace a sad face
on the glass with one damp hand until
the cashier pulls coins out of her purse,
saying if it is for you, take it. If it is for you.
And seeing us, the cashier smiles again,
though her face changes a bit while she pulls
at her smock, as if the gaps on the shelves
cannot be helped—for they cannot be helped,
no less than the confusion of pesos and dollars
in our pockets, or the fluorescent light on our skin—
yes, she says, transformed, something for you?

Something less than a mile away your cousins
have bought meat and cheese at the butcher's,
and Maricela, right now, pounds pepper and garlic,
carves plates of cabbage, lime, tomato, onion.
She pours mango juice and ice into fat
cobalt-rimmed glasses that she wraps in newspaper
to send with us when we blunder and admire
them aloud. Bali and Cesar show us
their room, bare but for Nirvana posters,
bunk beds, and new blue paint, they take us outside,
while the table is set and the milk crates
in the other rooms are emptied for chairs,
to show us Nana's old house up the way
where mint and heather, intertwined everywhere,
have taken over the doorway—as if enchanted—
and the neighbors and their children and others
we don't know come into the little three-roomed
house to eat, to talk, to see what we have brought
fearfully across with us in the backpacks
we carry. We exchange gifts. No no keep it.
They try out their English. Mortar

and pestle. Salsa is salsa. The table.
The souvenir. They laugh. The dogs.
The flies. Perros y moscas. Daring. Following
the scent of feasting from the open windows.

THREE

But you see, señores, this is how myth is made—

from just these shards—

this, this is historia.

—H. G. Carrillo

The Keepsake Storm

Keep

Alaska, late summer, *an octopus*
among the rocks, you write, its tentacles swaying
in the current near the skiff. Dead,
and in death, a gray suddenness
taking form, its unseeing arms cast into the untroubled movement
of your statement, where the depths threaten
but on no account surface:
ugly, like a plastic bag, nothing more to see, we got underway.

There are lapses in your wake, and even
so, momentum. I've strapped you
into the wheelchair. Hip surgery, morphine nights, the necessary
bedpan, you forget, and in forgetting, heave
at the belt with memory moving
only in the current, all arms suddenly roused. I'm off for a walk,
you say at breakfast, lifting your plate,
authorial yet,

as the woman who piloted her boat
one night through tall reefs
looming from beneath,
leadline, phosphorescent light, peering, channeling towards
the land mass merging with the darkness of sky and sea,

expertly,

and I'd like to talk to the management
this minute, you say,

anticipating highballs
of glacier ice, sweet, crystalline, fished from the bay,

but I am the management. This is who we are
together: you, counting tiles with your one
good eye, eyeing me as you labor
against referring to me to know who you are, and I,
with a knife and plastic bag
smashing two slugs of Valium into your ice cream
as if to brush these things aside, even mournfully,

in service to you, altogether too much
a prosthetic operation, the glove of the octopus
having fathomed how it wandered off point
onto shore, where you brought it, shifting
with forgetting and stillness, into being.

Qualifications

The night nurse restrained you in your bed
where you sleep without knowing we sit in all
evening reading the years of your ship's logs: the tip of Prince
of Wales Island a craggy, grasping hand
weathered down to veins and tendons,
the swell announcing every rock and reef
along the cape—

what hold it has on us

each of us, the hired help whom you call Barbara, who
it turns out, is a sister-in-law, frothing up
indiscriminately like the others not chronicled—
Dorothy, Mary,

Portland where you met
Stockton, and *Romany* the first of eighteen boats
from the yacht club Stockton purchased
as the Depression receded—

what do we know, knowing what we're told—

the hand seizing more cheerfully on a fashionable
young woman in a fussy hat, gloves, and heels,
returned from a luncheon to her motorized float
leaping forward in a start, dying, leaping forward,
dying, before, through binoculars,
you watched her row toward home,

envious, perhaps, with the mean hope
that her husband would someday be similarly stranded,
alone, in the astonishing grip of obstacles,

engines,

you came to know on your own: Cleo
was a hurricane in the backdrop of your divorce. We found
Stockton's note (Me, miserable. You too?)
folded into the logs, St. Croix for Alaska. He left you
the boat for a younger woman, so you hired
a hand and left him the islands, like so many qualified, isolated
    belongings.
A lady's glove drops, strokes the water's surface
and is sucked down into the deep where it moves,
feelered, unthinking, alien.

Minute

Aug. 22, 1964,
                    hurricane Cleo
heading this way—due Sunday 115 mph—
Decided sail St. Thomas tonight.
F. continued drinking till quite woozy
when we went down at 10:30—
His packing all over boat and not ready for sailing
and he wanting start immediately.
K. did not want to get in before daylight.
Engine batteries flat—F. had not checked—
K. exploded when finally broke thermos—
F. slept till 11:30 and still sodden
but got sail up and jumped engine start
from 32v. Strong winds & seas
but good angle. F. insisted on motor sailing.
K. slept till St. T. in sight

slowed engine speed to get in in daylight.
Anchor down 0600—Both slept
till 0730 then F. gone—Much difficulty
before K. finally got P. to help get sails down
& preparation made for Cleo—everybody
frantically leaving & working themselves.
K. finally to Henry for night
but Cleo passed 60 miles south of St. X—

Keel

Your boat, your cabin, your bed. This is your
agreed contract, the framework of the whole
wedded to the breastbone. You are the auxiliaries
working to preserve the heart: first mate,
ship's cook, oars if need be, seals you choose because
you are not the frame, but a projection

of the frame. And with what longing you sprung
from its side and followed, and also with courage, which,
you are reminded, is not among your strengths.
Your strength would have seen what promise lies
within, all but the ashtrays fastened down, yes, but
the frame, a delicate deal.
                You promise?
Yes. I promise, came the sun, came the throb
at her liver. Yes, sunup, and us. Without him.
And not really just that. The vast emerald bruise.
The child in the wheel. The years cold as gold,
and the machine in the sky, what else, sprung on itself.

Face

Here osteoporosis is imperceptible. Kathryn, 1942, slaps a brush
    against the hull of a boat, one arm cased in shadow,
    one arrested, flawless, in light. Not a ghost, not quite
    extinct, though plainly visible, cupped and pressed like this,

her bare back in a halter, her hair tangled in a wrap,
    the rigging snaked around her foothold on the pier,
    and above her, the mast nailing the sky: a pinpoint
    specimen in the annals of heaven, you joke, which is

more than I can say here on the sofa, where in rare form
    you remember: that's the *Romany*. We stripped her down,
    gave her a new look. Before that, I wanted horses, before I wanted
    a man who wanted to live on a boat. There is a word for what brings

you to face your own gaze the same as it leaves, dividing us further,
    dividing you from you and me, serenely, as your head
    nods against your shoulder and you lapse into absence.
    This is the side you lean on, where the eye is swollen shut.

Your spine, so curved, turns back on its origin. A word: not memory,
    nor ghost. Not spirit. Something in the tide of your will, some
    obsessive motion on some self-effacing residual path. I rinsed ants from
    your patio bricks. Still the trails that lead them back home.

Salt

When, from a distance, a cannery and a friendly cluster of homes
    came into view from the boat, nothing much
happened. Just the familiar imperceptible way
    of the brackish mind stirring in the scene, the scene crystallizing:
gardens in tangles, doors padlocked or hanging drunkenly,
    the beach a junkyard of boilers: abandoned.
And disappointment, but realization too, as one surface
    dissolves into another, freezes, or seems to freeze—

a woman at the foot of a woman, changing her socks.
    She tugs from the heel, the sock gives inside-out, flakes
of skin float in the air. Over the nails she rubs ointment, over
    the bone where it weeps with infection. Nothing prepares
you for clarity when it comes, not from elusive memory
    or long study, but from a small approximating
accident of choice, happenstance, the right variables cross, in spite of
    endless training in watchfulness: if you don't know

ask: towels, here, wipes, here. How to make her coffee mostly milk,
    how to scramble her eggs with cream, how to
cut to bits, to salt, to bib and spoon, to line the blanket
    in case of accidents (she spills on purpose)—lift this way,
never from the front. Mind her close, she's had too many
    falls, you'll see in the nurse's log, where, by the way,
you must record your shift. And take care. Take care: that salient
    gesticulation at the close of each log signaling

that some care is taken for granted, care of one's self, one's position:
    one's taking care against taking responsibility or blame,
against the briny tentacles of weariness and fear, which
    in a moment—waking on her own to ask for the toilet, trip

number five, her foot torn open in the careless wheel—take us
both down into the wreck where we lay siege to its
inscrutability, where I am she is enveloped in translucent
elementals: abandon, abandon: one for another.

Shift

Ants and the vacuum cleaner,
point and counter,
already made ridiculous

by my routine of killing
time by keeping order:
pills, meals, laundering

the long hours between
now and the end of this
shift. In time of course

I talk to myself, for talking
to you is simply too much
the same act as that mad

preoccupation between
me and the damned ants, who
are incidental in all

this getting nowhere better
business. Still in your nightie,
that loose cotton shift I am

to change to presentable
clothing in the morning,
you talk to the ants

on the carpet. Do you
like my dress? Fire! Fire!
The babies! Two witnesses:

not a dress but a nightgown,
not babies but ants—the fire?
Yes, I see the fire taking

everything. Antarctica?
So vast you can never
see the same place twice.

Ice

I've seen so many things put carefully away—

Because I've been shelving
the breakfast plates, this is my beginning.

Other ways in: pick a photograph.
Kathryn naked in the grass,
Kathryn's husband trims her hair on deck,
Kathryn stands in a lifejacket
calling an albatross from the ice floes.

Pick a map. Beneath the ice,
West Antarctica is an island archipelago.
There, the Virgin Islands. There's the Oregon coast.
Today is a summer day in the Arizona desert.
Describe the days breaking away from their season.
Say we make them up as we go.

We might get us early to bed, she says
to one of her husbands, maybe,

years of yachts on the separated seas
leaning on the breeze—
a woman pressed against a rail, starboard—

It might just end there,
extravagant, ablaze.

Or start now, begin with now,
the summer guest house,
the feeble mind, the cups of milk

she calls her cocktails.
It's a hundred and five degrees out.
Below her porch, the cracked clay waits on rain,
or any such element of connection.

Think you'll rouse
something from the shelves?

Flip through the imperative albums.

In the beginning—
two sailors, a storm——-

Turn the pages forward, back.
Greenland, Alaska, both Poles.
No telling ice from ice.
Adjust her neck brace: who's this hanging around my neck?

K and Me
On the Porch
Circa 5pm

Winter forgotten, wrens visit the feeder.
They come, beaks gaping and silent,
insolent because they come thirsty.

The only noise is the flies' contempt
for our presence on the porch, our first
outdoor spring today. It's hot. I seat her

in the shade to shade her from August.
Above us, the clouds break down, water
evaporates in the summer heat, consents.

We name the birds hanging at the feeder.
A grasshopper harvests the quiet.
Done for, we fall for it all, resistant.

Telling

No sign of human occupancy. Silence. Wilderness. In the telling, nothing
intelligible, nothing written there: high tide, the inland lagoon stippled

with rock protrusions, tiny islands of grass, flooded shrubbery,
the chart's only navigable channel alleging markers by now submerged

in silty waters, and no discernible way back: a little juncture
in the record leaving off here, unfinished, the thought called away

by more urgent events, I guess, which is to imply some essential
difference between experience and myth I don't mean: the writer leaves

her book behind. Still the natives raise their burial houses and totems
where in the hollows of the carving weather leaves the paint intact.

Still the dead are hung from bathroom walls, hyacinths and tulips,
photographs taken by her second husband who discovered

how to x-ray fine-line cracks in steel bridges, but died shortly after.
Family legacy: Robert Oppenheimer, isn't it true, on the islands

listening to radio news in 1960, sipping cocktails with Stockton
and Kathryn. Not only the most visible markers or unadorned

juxtapositions—the ring she still wears, the third husband,
Tibet, China, the Asiatic Sea—still becoming legible, habitable,

but also living evidence among the monuments, the telling portion:
at seventy-nine, alone, she bought a house.

1909–1996

Nearly 88, infinity next to infinity,
but infinity curled on itself, a whirlwind
that whipped about the house and was gone,
rain in its wake, a smell of dirt.
A woman leans against pillows, yawns,
and recalls herself over her writing:
—*Hurricane Cleo heading this way*—
the man she'd hired circled the deck,
inebriated, the sea slapped the hull
in the night, hung from the sides,
sliming the deck with spray.
Help over here, I said, will you help—
She looks down at her wedding ring,
says to someone in the kitchen
—*shall we announce our anniversary?*
But she'd meant to connect this thought
to hurricane Cleo headed this way—
I've seen so many rings put carefully away—
and she notices her feet are slippered, but cold,
though it looks like summer outside the door,
summers in Antarctica, winters on St. Croix,
islands upon islands giving way to more islands,
or the still blank surface of the door's glass pane.
—*I keep thinking I'm going to get up
better than before,* but that isn't the way
the seasons of things travel. What was it
she's forgotten? Promises, she made promises—
I can hold it together at a word. *A word with you, please?*
I'm an old sailor, *let me tell you a story*—
it's like rousing the dead, like burying the living.
We had to get the sails down, fold ourselves in,
though there's no preparation for the storm.

Cleaving

1. lean as a fossil, hazard, rare,

2. cacophonous, no doubt. Decay.

3. A woman kneels
    at a woman's feet and changes her
    socks. She tugs the blue terry from the long heel,
    and the sock yields inside-out.
    The wound, weeks old, weeps openly

4. indeterminate as the pronouns themselves

5. the last leg up, the demand of evidence,
    what you must see,

6. the ragged voices of also the wrens
    become the sudden house
    and dwell beyond us,
    the interval between, the cleaving

7. leaning on the increments: she, me,

8. this, the kitchen,
    the bedroom and the lidded cup,
    the curtains drawn against the sun,
    this humpback bed. Latex gloves.

9. Practically anything
    one might bridge
    with utterance:

10.   the small desert from out the glass door works like a sea

11.   to pieces she recovers.

Archaeopteryx, an Elegy

As soon as possible, I will confront the wren's
        doings, rinse the white streaks from the porch bricks
drawing lizards from their shade, the immediate
        smell of water too much for all of us.
But first is lunch. The remains we'll scatter over
        the driveway away from the bricks. Wrens come,
crusts from our dishes make drama. Then history.

What is possible in memory is disingenuous.
        Limestone, impressed with the archaic smile
of bone and reptilian wrists, wishbones and feathers,
        describes. It cups the transitional form,
naturally selecting one's best side. There was
        the time you forgot your legs no longer
could recall how to stand—then rose up straight and sang

        You'll come a-waltzing Matilda with me

Probably I've been thinking of that since August.
        The indelible wrens grate like shovels
outside—exhumed, one voice rises from wilderness,
        echoes,
                settles, rests
                    —then another, and,
between them, the keep of an unerring quiet.

Acknowledgments

Grateful acknowledgment is made to the editors of the following magazines and publications in which these poems originally appeared:

The Black Warrior Review: "Fishing"
The Chattahoochee Review: "Through the Glass" first appeared as "Revelation"
Crazyhorse: "The Spirit that Appears When You Call"
The Georgia Review: "That Cried to the Whole City 'Sleep No More'"
The G. W. Review: "That He Will Land and Find His Feet" first appeared as "Scared Darren on a Tree Branch above the River"
Loft and Range: A Poetry Anthology: "Velvet," "Through the Glass," "These Years, in the Deepest Holes," "Couldn't I Want to Be a Man, Sometimes," "Where the Bodies, Half-Dressed, in Pieces," and "The Bells," which appeared as "Sunday Morning"
Mosaic: "Del Rio"
Prairie Schooner: "Their Lives and Shadows"

I would like to thank Meg Files for her tireless encouragement, backbone, and good words. To Pam Barnes and Frank Gaspar: wow and thank you. For their faith and help, I also want to thank Archie Ammons, Alice Fulton, Roger Gilbert, Michael Gorra, Karl Kirchwey, Robert Morgan, Steve Orlen, Helena Maria Viramontes, and especially Dorothy Mermin and Reeve Parker. I am indebted to Karen Anderson and Jasper Bernes for sincere criticism and enthusiasm, and to Dina Bishara for support. To Herman Carrillo: sólo contigo. To Laura Van Etten, my keeper, thanks again.

"The Walk Like Old Habits" is for Sara Antonia Li. The title of "That Cried to the Whole City 'Sleep No More'" quotes Wordsworth's Prelude, Book X, lines 75–76. "Where it Goes" is Leslie's poem. "The Keepsake Storm" is for Kathryn H. Bishop.

About the Author

Gina Franco was born in Clifton-Morenci, Arizona, where she lived until the Phelps Dodge mine strike of 1983 concluded with the permanent breakup of the unions and the flooding of the San Francisco River in Clifton. She has since lived intermittently in Tucson, Arizona, where for several years she wrote, worked, and attended Pima Community College. In 1995, she left the Southwest for Northampton, Massachusetts, where she completed her B.A. in English at Smith College as an Ada Comstock Scholar. Currently she lives in Ithaca, New York, an M.F.A./Ph.D. candidate at Cornell University. She holds an M.F.A. in poetry writing and an M.A. in English from Cornell, where she teaches in the John S. Knight Institute for Writing in the Disciplines, and where her writing and teaching have received a number of awards. Her creative work has appeared in various literary journals. She will be an assistant professor of English at Knox College in Galesburg, Illinois.

Library of Congress Cataloging-in-Publication Data
Franco, Gina L.
The keepsake storm : poems / by Gina Franco.
p. cm. — (Camino del sol)
ISBN 0-8165-2329-0 (pbk. : alk. paper)
1. Mexican-American Border Region—Poetry. 2. Arizona—Poetry.
I. Title. II. Series
PS3606.R375 K44 2004
811'.6—dc21
2003010222